To

Richard B[...]

Merry Christmas
From
Hill Tire Co.
And

Ludlow
Coombs

WHO CARES
ABOUT APATHY?

WHO CARES ABOUT APATHY?

Ludlow Porch

 Peachtree Publishers, Ltd.

Published by
Peachtree Publishers, Ltd.
494 Armour Circle, N.E.
Atlanta, Georgia 30324

Manufactured in the United States of America

10 9 8 7 6 5 4 3 2 1

Library of Congress Catalog Card Number 87-80972

ISBN 0-934601-30-5

For Esther, the friend I never knew.

Contents

Who cares about apathy?

A Lot Of Bread, A Little Meat

The human mind is a wonderful thing, especially its ability to hold on to the good or funny things that happen to us and to block out the rest. I guess that's God's way of making sure that most of our memories are good ones.

If you want to test this theory, just listen sometime when an old-timer starts talking about the Great Depression. His eyes will twinkle with just a touch of pride — pride that he gained by "making it" through those awful years. Time has softened his memories.

Old Man Wilson loved to tell stories about the Depression. He was in his element when he could be in the middle of a crowd, smoking his pipe and reminiscing about "The Hoover Days." His stories always started the same way:

"Yes, sir, things were sure tight in 1933. I remember one time my daddy could have bought a forty-acre farm for two dollars. The bank was gonna lend him the money, but the poor old thing couldn't come up with the down payment.

"I remember the time they took up collection at church. All they got was two apples, a broke King Hardware knife, and an I.O.U. for forty cents from the richest man in town. Yea, times were sho tough.

"You know, money was so tight that the Ku Klux Klan couldn't afford sheets; had to wrap toilet paper all over themselves. Silliest lookin' things you ever saw. Fire hazard, too, what with them always burnin' crosses and things.

"Never would have been no gol dang Depression, hadn't of been for Hoover. I knew from the start that he was a bad apple. You could tell it by lookin' at him. You know what I mean. He looked right funny out of his eyes. Yeah, old Hoover was just one of them rich Republicans, never worked a day in his life; wouldn't know a mule from a sack of Bull Durham.

"You think 1933 was tough? You should have been around in '32. My God in Heaven, was times bad. You might not believe it, but it was so tough in '32 the Chattahoochee River didn't run but three days a week.

"Seven kids in my family. We had to really scratch to feed that crowd. Mama used to always say take a big bite of bread and a little bite of meat. She used to make them great big old cat head biscuits. She called 'em that because they was a big as a cat's head. Daddy raised hogs, and believe me, we didn't waste nothin'. We ate everything from the snout to the tail. What I'm tryin' to tell you is, we ate everything but the oink.

"Yes sir, damn Republicans. Hadn't been for President Roosevelt, we would have all starved to death. One thing on earth I can't abide is a damned shifty-eyed Republican. Why, I tell you straight out, I ain't got no use for 'em till this day. Why, I'd rather have a sister in a whore house than a brother in the Republican Party.

"Poor? You wanna know how poor we was? Last three kids my mama and daddy had, they couldn't even afford to give 'em a middle name."

It was at about this point in Mr. Wilson's story that he would pause, take a long draw on his pipe, and then continue in a much softer voice:

"You know what, though? Lookin' back on it, I'm not so sure we was so bad off. We generally had enough to eat. It was usually them cat head biscuits with streak-o-lean and milk gravy, but hell, that wasn't so bad. As a matter of fact, I'd give my paid-up Metropolitan policy for one of Mama's biscuits right now.

"In those days, folks seemed to care more about each other. Families stuck together. You seldom if ever heard about a divorce. Couldn't nobody I know afford a lawyer.

"And kids were more respectful to their elders. There was no dope in the schools and no income tax to speak of. We didn't worry about nuclear war, and it only cost a dime to go to the picture show.

"Yeah, lookin' back on the Great Depression, I don't reckon it was all that bad."

Like I said before, the human mind is a wonderful thing.

When The Rubber Became A Condom

I guess you could call me old-fashioned. I still long for the days when banana splits cost thirty cents and every little boy in America wanted to grow up to look like Charles Atlas and act like Jack Armstrong.

I miss those summer days when I could pedal my bike all day and never get tired. Those were the days when the print in telephone books was larger and the national debt was smaller.

The thing I miss most, however, is the innocence.

It was a time when no one said "damn" or "hell" in mixed company, when girls who smoked in public were considered "fast," and when you had to go to France if you wanted to see a bikini.

In those innocent days, certain things were just not discussed in polite society. Case in point: the condom.

In the south of the forties and fifties, they were not even called condoms; we called them "rubbers." We were not so innocent that we didn't know all about them, but we were convinced that it would be social suicide to let any adult discover that we knew of their existence. In fact, I was convinced for many years that many adults didn't know they existed.

Every teen-aged boy knew two things for sure about rubbers: (1) They would prevent disease. We knew that because it said right on the package in big red letters, "Sold for the prevention of disease only;" (2) They would prevent babies. Nobody told us that; we just knew it.

Neither of these, however, was the reason teen-aged boys bought rubbers. We never expected to use them. At that age and at that time, we felt very lucky if we got to kiss a girl good night. We carried them because doing so was one of the things expected of teen-aged boys by their peers. It was considered the natural order. We loved our mamas, we loved Franklin Delano Roosevelt, and we loved Joe Louis (in spite of the fact that he beat up white men on a more or less regular basis). And last, but not least, we were expected to carry a rubber in our wallet.

In our young minds, it was the ultimate sign of manhood. It was perfectly acceptable to have no driver's license or social security card, but to have no telltale circle showing in your wallet was a flagrant, silent admission that you were not a *real* American, did not love John Wayne or remember Pearl Harbor. It was clear evidence that you were afraid to beat up a queer, and that when all was said and done, your heart pumped pee-pee.

A trip to the drugstore to buy rubbers could be so traumatic that it could alter your personality for life. You would walk up to the drugstore and peer in the window, all the time praying that no customers were there.

Once you had satisfied yourself that the druggist was alone, it was okay to go in.

It was not, however, the time to make your purchase. You needed more time to screw up your courage. You would go to the comic book rack and thumb through a Captain Marvel or a Mickey Mouse. After several minutes, you would stand as tall as possible and walk quickly and with great confidence to the counter. When the druggist said, "Can I help you?" you avoided eye contact and said very matter of factly, "I'd like a pack of Dentyne, a Hershey bar, two Trojans and a bottle of Vitalis hair tonic." The druggist would grin broadly as he filled the order. He probably had done the same thing some years before.

Although we never, and I mean *never*, expected to use them, we all lied about it. Tales of conquests were as common as pimples. But the fact of the matter is that millions and millions of rubbers dry rotted in our wallets. Peer pressure did not require that we ever use them, just that we owned them.

In those days before the sexual revolution, merely displaying a condom in our wallet was enough to show the world that, should the opportunity arise, we were ready. Dear God, were we ready!

I hadn't thought much about rubbers in years. Then, the other day, the Surgeon General announced that they would help stop disease. Think about that for a moment. The Surgeon General of our entire United States of America called a press conference to tell the nation what every teen-aged boy in this country had known since the age of thirteen. For me, his announcement seemed to mark the end of the sexual revolution.

I was also struck with this simple realization: Somewhere in this great country, in a long-forgotten, long-lost junkyard, rests the remains of a rusting 1940 Ford coupe with two Trojans taped discreetly under the dashboard.

Thanks to AIDS, herpes, and the Surgeon General of the United States, the sexual revolution seems to be over. And I never fired a shot.

What Price Victory?

I pride myself on reading the newspaper everyday, and, generally speaking, I think I have a glimmer of understanding of what's going on in the world around me. There is, however, one thing that just absolutely puzzles me.

The President and the Congress have been fussing about aid to the Nicaragua contras for a long time. What I don't understand is, once we decide to give fifty or a hundred million dollars to these folks, how do we get it to them?

I've seen TV pictures of the contras. Now, these folks are living in the jungle, sleeping on the ground. I'm sure that not a one of them could come up with three credit references. With this in mind, how in the name of Rambo do we get the money to the contras? Do we give them the hundred million in the form of a government check? I doubt it. Who's going to cash a hundred million dollar check for an old boy with no ID, wearing a camouflage suit and carrying an automatic weapon?

Okay, let's say that some way or another they

are able to get the check cashed, and now they're walking around the jungle carrying a hundred million dollars. What are they going to do with it? They can't go to town because the government troops are waiting there to kill them. They can't make purchases by mail order 'cause there ain't no place to mail a letter in the jungle.

Even if they managed to slip into town, I've got to wonder what they'd do when they get there. How many places do you think there are in Nicaragua where you can buy weapons? Is there a place called Fred's Tank Store? Can you get a good buy on surface-to-air missiles at Ace Hardware?

I wonder what would happen if they took all that cash and offered to buy the government from the Sandinistas. Don't laugh. I bet it would be easier than trying to get a hundred million dollar money order cashed at a 7-11 store in downtown Managua.

Bopping At The Hops

The first time Ronny ever tasted beer, he was not yet two years old. He was sitting in his father's lap and was allowed to suck the foam off the top of a can of Pabst Blue Ribbon. He smacked his little lips and clapped his hands together wildly. Everyone in the room knew that even at that tender age, as far as baby Ronny was concerned, it was love at first suck.

That love affair goes on to this day, even after the passing of more than forty summers.

Ronny's parents soon learned that any beer left around on a coffee table was fair game for the beer guzzling toddler. When Ronny was five, he was left in the care of an elderly baby sitter for the evening. She dozed off on the sofa, and while she slept, Ronny discovered a six-pack of beer in the refrigerator. He made very short work of all six bottles. When his parents returned about midnight, they found the baby sitter still sleeping. Ronny was sitting in front of the television, holding what was left of the last beer. With horror in her voice, his mother screamed,

"Ronny, what are you doing?" Smiling a drunken little smile, Ronny said, "Nothing much Mommie. I'm just watching that asshole Superman on television."

Ronny got himself in and out of the usual teen-age scrapes, most of which included excessive beer drinking. He drank his way through West Georgia College, where he set beer drinking records that some folks say will stand longer than the great pyramids. He was expelled three times, all for his antics after a case or two of beer.

On one occasion, he painted the local Tastee Freeze drive-in black. It was not a real good job, but he was so proud that he insisted on signing his work.

It took him six years, but by some miracle Ronny managed to graduate from college. The joke around the campus was that he had graduated *magna cum Lowenbrau*.

Ronny became moderately successful in business, in spite of the fact that by his mid twenties he was averaging about a case of beer a night.

When Ronny married Beth, it was in spite of the fact that she did not drink and did not like it much when he did. She was, however, by nature a right tolerant old girl and didn't complain much at first. She rationalized Ronny's excess by saying that he only drank beer, never missed work, and, after all, it was his only hobby.

By the time our hero was thirty-five, he was drinking more beer than a trainload of winos. It was not at all uncommon for Ronny to drink two cases of beer a night and then sing himself to sleep in front of the TV.

Beth's patience was, by now, wearing very thin. She was nagging and they were fighting more and more.

One Friday night, Ronny came home drunker than a three-eyed goat. Beth met him at the back door. He was laughing at the top of his lungs and singing, "When the Roll Is Called Up Yonder, I'll Be There." She said, "Ron, you should be ashamed! How much have you had to drink?"

Laughing wildly, he said, "I don't know for sure, but when I left, the bartender gave me a ham, and on the way home, I heard on the car radio that Budweiser stock was up five points."

She said through clinched teeth, "Get back in that car, Ronald. I'm going to show you something."

"Are you crazy? It's two o'clock in the morning."

"Get back in that car and do it this minute," Beth said, "or I'll make you wish you had died as a small child." Ron knew by the tone of her voice that his interests would be best served by doing as he was told. Beth pushed the empty beer cans out of the driver's seat and slid under the wheel. Still laughing, Ronny got in the front seat beside her.

"Where are we going, Sugarlips?" Ron asked.

"Never mind, I'll tell you when I get there."

She drove outside of town to a hilltop overlooking the town's large brewery. The brewery was a beehive of activity. All the lights were blazing and smoke was rolling out of the giant chimneys. A long freight train was rolling into the brewery grounds and semis were pulling out, loaded down with thousands of cases of beer. Three forklifts were busy going back and forth loading a fourth semi. Beth turned to Ron, who had stopped laughing and was licking his lips as he saw all of that wonderful beer being made. In a loud, accusing voice, Beth said, "Do you see that, Ron? Do you see that? They can make beer a lot faster than you can drink it."

Ron, suddenly sober and serious, looked Beth right in the eye and said, "Yeah, that may be true, but by God, I got 'em working nights."

The Old Barber Shop

If you're not careful, it is very easy to blink twice and lose part of your childhood. A case in point is the family barber shop.

In this day of unisex hair styling salons, it's difficult to remember your old neighborhood barber shop. It was the center for most of the good sportstalk. Elections could be forecast in advance if you would just keep your ears open any Saturday afternoon before election day. You could find every old magazine ever printed, and if you got there early enough, you could look in the sports page and get the box score of last night's Atlanta Crackers baseball game.

They say you can't go home and I believe that. However, that doesn't stop me from daydreaming. There is not much I wouldn't give for just one more visit.

I'd walk down Main Street, and about one block before I got there, I'd see the red and white barber pole turning slowly. I'm closer now; I just went past East Point Ford Company with those wonderful shiny old Fords on the showroom floor. I'm close enough now to make out the sign on the big plate-glass window, and it says in big white letters, "Abe and Bud's Barber Shop." I pull open the screen door and step inside.

Standing behind the first chair is Abe. It's just like I remembered. He has someone in his chair and is holding a comb in one hand and scissors in the other. When he sees me, he says, "Come on in, Luddy, it won't be long." I move past his chair and take a seat.

From the second barber chair, Bud looks up and says, "Where you been? We heard you was in jail!" Everyone laughs. Sam is holding forth in the third chair. Quieter than Abe or Bud, he just looks at me, nods his head and smiles.

There are three men ahead of me, so I reach for a magazine on the table beside. I have about four choices: *Ring* magazine, *Look*, *True Detective*, or the *Police Gazette*. I thumb through a story in *Ring* about a new boxer fresh from the Olympics named Floyd Patterson. Abe is shaving the back of his customer's neck with a straight razor and explaining that the Atlanta Crackers are never going to win another Southern Association pennant until their owner, Earl Mann, stops selling players anytime he can make a ten dollar profit.

The big fan at the back of the shop is slowly moving back and forth, while the two overhead fans are turning slowly. The whole place smells like talcum powder and Vitalis. The shine boy is

sweeping up hair. The radio behind Bud is playing a Hank Williams song. An old man sticks his
head in the front door and asks, "How many in
front of me, Abe?" Abe smiles and says, "You
ain't got nothin' better to do. Come on in and
wait." Everybody laughs again.

It was a great, wonderful place to go, "Abe and
Bud's." Friendly, warm, wonderful men; barbers
and customers alike.

I guess they're right. You can never go home.
Dammit, they're right.

Out Of The Mouths Of Babies

When you host a talk show on the radio, your whole life revolves around the next topic. There are a number of questions you need to answer before you settle on one:

1. Is it of general interest to your audience?
2. Will it generate interesting, informative or funny telephone calls?
3. Where will the calls lead you? Will your topic produce vulgar or racist calls?
4. The most important question is, Will this topic entertain your audience?

Over the years, the one topic that has never let me down is one I call, "Out of the Mouths of Babies."

Children say great, funny, wise things, and almost everyone has at least one thing that their children, grandchildren or relatives have come out with. Sometimes they're funny, sometimes embarrassing, but always entertaining.

One of my all-time favorite "out of the mouths of babies" was called in by a little boy's mother. The child had been raised next door to his aunt, and he visited her every day, in spite of the fact that he was only a shade past his fourth birthday. Living so close, his aunt had become almost a second mother to him. When his aunt died, everyone agreed that the child was too young to fully grasp what had happened. On the day of the funeral, the youngster insisted that he be allowed to go to his beloved aunt's funeral. His mother was reluctant but finally agreed. Everything went smoothly at the church. The child was well behaved and, all in all, was a perfect little man. When the minister completed his graveside services, the family hung around talking and consoling each other. They were still there when the men came to fill the grave. When the first shovel full of dirt was thrown in, the mourners got very quiet. When the third shovel full of dirt hit bottom, the silence was broken by the four-year-old. He said, "Well, I guess that's the last we'll see of her."

Then there was the call from the daddy of a three-year-old boy. Like most three-year-olds, he was convinced that the place to spend the night was in the bed with his mother and father. He would start off the night in his own bed, but sometime before daylight, he managed to wind up in the bed with his parents. They knew it was not a good thing for the development of a three-year-old, and they tried every trick in the book: "Big boys sleep alone;" "Three year olds are too big to sleep with us;" "Your toys will be so lonely;" "Superman sleeps by himself."

Little by little, they seemed to be gaining on the problem. It was obvious from talking to the child that he wanted to be able to sleep alone. He tried, but at two o'clock in the morning, the temptation to jump into Mom and Dad's safe, warm bed was just too much to resist.

One day, Daddy got the word from his boss that he had to go out of town to the home office for two weeks. When he came home, the entire family was at the airport to meet him. It was crowded, as the Atlanta airport always is. The three-year-old's eyes searched the faces of the deplaning passengers until he finally saw his father. He broke away and started running full tilt toward his father, yelling at the top of his lungs "Daddy, Daddy, Mommie didn't sleep with anyone while you were gone!"

I don't think any of us really understand how literal children can be. They take most things they hear as Gospel truth, until age and experience teach them better. Take, for instance, a story told by one of my callers.

His little boy had just discovered how to wiggle out of his high chair. When he was finished with his meal, or when the meal simply didn't suit him, he would start his downward wiggle and in seconds be standing on the floor. His father decided it was time to nip this bad habit smack in the middle of the bud. When the rest of the family was barely midway through supper, our hero started to wiggle out of his high chair. In his best drill instructor voice, Daddy said, "Richard, stop that!" No response. Then he said, "Richard, stop that...one, two, three." On the count of three, he picked Richard up out of the chair and popped him about three licks on his backside. The family continued to eat.

In about three minutes, Richard started to wiggle again. The command was repeated: "Richard, stop that...one, two, three." He then picked him up and paddled his bottom again. Within ninety seconds, the procedure was repeated: "Richard, stop that...one, two, three," followed by the spanking. To Mama and Daddy's amazement, Richard stayed in the chair and finished eating with the rest of the family.

When it was time for Richard's bath, he was put in the tub with his brother to soak and play for a few minutes before the actual scrubbing started. Then Daddy heard screams from the bathroom and ran to the door. Richard was splashing water on his brother and all over the bathroom floor. In a loud voice, the father said, "Richard, stop that...one, two..." He never got to three. On the count of two, with a look of absolute horror on his face, Richard climbed quickly out of the tub, wet and naked as a catfish, ran straight to the kitchen and climbed into his high chair.

Age is a topic that will always catch the interest of the little folks. Children have their own ideas about what old is, what young is, and what a baby is.

The ultimate insult for a first grader is to call him a baby. A substitute teacher called to tell me this story.

She was trying to get to know the first graders she had been assigned to for the day. She went around the room asking each one questions and generally making small talk: "How old are you?" "How many brothers and sisters do you have?" "What do you want to be when you grow up?"

When she had talked to every child, she said, "Do you have any questions you'd like to ask me?" Instantly, a little boy in the back said, "Yeah, how old are you?" The teacher said, "I'm sixty-two years old." In a voice filled with pity, the little boy said, "Wow! You'll be dead meat soon."

Another caller told the story of the five-year-old who asked his grandmother how old she was. The grandmother replied that she was eighty-two. The child said, "Boy, Granma, you should have been dead years ago."

I think the reason stories about children are always popular is the fact that, for the most part, they are always honest. Children hug only when they feel like hugging, and they kiss only when they want to express an emotion. The thing that makes them God's greatest gift, however, is the fact that they never say they love you if they don't mean it.

Growing up is not all it's cracked up to be.

The Personals Column

One of my favorite parts of the newspaper is the Personals column. If you read them on a regular basis, they take on an almost soap opera quality.

I was reading the Personals column the other day and saw this one:

"I, John Eugene Beardon, will not be responsible for the debts of anyone except myself. Especially that south Georgia white trash by the name of Martha Mae that I married while I was drunk."

You just don't overlook an ad like that.

A few days later, I noticed this ad:

"John Eugene Beardon was not responsible for my debts while I was married to the gravy suckin' pig. As a matter of fact, he ain't never had a dime to his name. He has bad breath, a hammer toe deformity, and his mama wears a flea collar."

Two days later:

"Martha Mae, my mama is a saint, and you ain't fit to slop her hogs. I hope your tattoo fades. That's what I get for marrying double-wide white trash."

Two days later:

"John Eugene, if your mama is a saint, then grits ain't groceries. When that old woman dies, there ain't gonna be no place for her to go. She's meaner than a snake with a backache. If she didn't stay passed out drunk most of the time, couldn't nobody stand to be in the same county with her. I never particularly cared for her."

Three days later:

"Martha Mae, you got a real mean mouth. April 25, the day we got married, was the blackest day of my life. I hate your guts."

Two days later:

"Johnny, you remembered our anniversary. Thanks for the memories. Your little peach, Martha Mae."

Two days later:

"Dear, dear little peach, do you remember the Dixie Motel and the IHOP restaurant on our honeymoon in Panama City? It was heaven, Johnny. P.S. Mama sends her love."

That was the last time I read the Personals column. There was just no way that this was going to turn out all right.

Lardo Rides Again

I have written many times about my boyhood friend, Lardo Dupree. In case you don't remember Lardo, he is in business for himself. He is probably the world's leading writer of country and western song titles. Lardo's theory is a simple one, but it has made him rich: anyone can write a country western song, once he has a good title. Lardo, therefore, just writes and sells titles.

He called me the other day and invited me to come by and look at his new fall catalog. His titles are set up in the catalog according to subject matter. I've picked out a few of my favorites:

MAMA SONGS

My Sylacauga Mama
Mama Could Bench Press Loretta Lynn
Mama Kneed Santa on Christmas Eve
Don't Cross Mama When She's Drinkin' Bud

PATRIOTIC SONGS

Kadafy's Mama Wears a Flea Collar
Castro's Heart Pumps Pee-Pee

LOVE SONGS

Sit Me in a High Chair, Tie a Bib Around My
   Neck and Feed Me One More Lie
Kissin' You Makes My Eyes Cross
She Left Me Flat in Our Roll-Away Bed

In looking over Lardo's new fall catalog and
realizing that he depends on it for a living, I'm
struck with one thought . . . It's a wonder to me
that Lardo doesn't starve to death.

Kreeping Kudzu

I have heard several versions of how kudzu came to this country. The most widely accepted is that it was brought here from Japan in the 1930s. Somebody got the idea that since it grew so fast, it would not only stop soil erosion but would also furnish feed for cattle. Since that time, it has become the national vine of the South.

I don't know exactly how fast it grows; I guess that depends on the weather and the soil. I do know that there are a thousand stories about its speed.

For example, there is a mile-long dirt stock car track in south Georgia. The story goes that before the race cars could get all the way around the track, kudzu grew from a nearby field and four cars were lost for eight months.

Then, there's the story about kudzu and Jimmy Hoffa, but I never put much stock in that.

One day my friend Snake Burnett was working on his farm. He was standing waist-deep in a field of kudzu, spraying it with poison in a futile effort to reclaim his field. A car with Vermont license plates stopped and watched Snake as he was spraying the field. When curiosity got the best of the couple in the car, the man got out and walked to the edge of the field. He was wearing shorts with long black socks, wing-tip shoes and a flowered Hawaiian shirt.

The man said, "Pardon me, young fellow, but what is that lovely plant that you are fertilizing?"

Without missing a beat, Snake said, "This, sir, is the vine of the rare south Georgia orchid."

"I never heard of the south Georgia orchid."

"I told you its rare," Snake said. "As a matter of fact, they are so rare that only a few Saudi Arabian millionaires can afford them."

"Where are the blooms?" the man asked.

"Oh, they only bloom on legal holidays," Snake answered.

The man said, "I don't guess you would sell me some cuttings, would you?"

"I don't know," Snake said, "It's pretty expensive."

The man said, "Name your price."

"Well, I usually only sell it to select florists, but you look like a nice guy." Taking a deep breath, Snake went on, "I'll tell you what I'll do. I'll sell you a trunkload for three hundred dollars, but at that price, you'll have to pick it yourself. And you have to promise that you'll never tell anyone where you got it, cause my florist customers would be furious if they thought I was selling retail."

It took the couple about thirty minutes to pull up a trunkload of kudzu. While the man was handing Snake three one-hundred-dollar bills, Snake asked, "Where you folks from?" The man said they were from West Jackson, Vermont. The story goes that the couple went right back home and planted that whole trunkload of kudzu.

I know what you're thinking . . . that you never heard of West Jackson, Vermont. Now, you know why.

Wit & Wisdom From Ludlow

❝I make it a point never to use the word 'whom'. If you use it properly, you sound pretentious. If you use it improperly, you sound stupid.❞

*

❝Negative people are all buried in unmarked graves.❞

*

❝Ignorance is like concrete. The longer it stays, the tougher it is to get rid of.❞

The One-Eyed Thief

In the past ten years, I have been involved in a love-hate relationship with television. First, the love.

TV has brought instant, around-the-world news coverage to our lives. It has made it possible for folks from Seattle to Miami to be at the World Series and on the fifty-yard line at the Super Bowl. It allowed us to be in Dallas on that dark day when Lee Harvey Oswald wrote his name in our history books. It has allowed us all to see the Olympics, live. It has made us many new friends, from Barney Fife to Huntley and Brinkley. It has brought us much joy, entertainment and, from time to time, some education. So much for the love.

TV has also stolen much from us. Today's children, huddled around the TV set, are missing something that every previous generation has enjoyed — the magic of childhood imagination. How long has it been since you saw a child playing with that most wonderful of all toys, an empty refrigerator box? It could be an airplane, a submarine or a spaceship. Children don't need to do that anymore. They can see real space ships on TV.

Some of the best summer days of my life were spent in the company of Captain Marvel, Spider-man, Plastic Man and Batman. If you could scrape up a dime, you could buy your favorite comic book. When you finished reading about your hero, you could trade it to a friend and on and on. TV killed the comic book as sure as a hog gives ham.

TV also killed marbles, kite flying and root-de-peg. TV killed kick-the-can, hopscotch, and paper dolls. It killed skinny dipping, dirt clod battles, and drive-in movies. It killed follow the leader, leap frog, and capture the flag.

Television's biggest crime, however, is that children don't read for fun anymore. That is truly, truly sad. It is sad because future generations of children will never be able to pole a raft down the Mississippi with Tom and Huck. They will never be with Jim Hawkins on Treasure Island, and they will never walk the moors with Holmes and Watson.

I just hope the next time we sit down to watch TV, we really enjoy it. It better be good. We have paid a big price for it.

Bubba Of The Boilermakers

Of all the characters I've ever met, Bubba is without a doubt the most interesting and outrageous. Bubba is six feet, two inches tall and his weight generally runs 400-425 pounds. He is a wonderful cook, and he eats every meal like he just escaped from a P.O.W. camp.

He is probably the only man I have ever known who can draw a crowd just to watch him eat. He has a large walrus-like mustache. I point this out so you can get a better picture of how Bubba eats chicken. He picks up the chicken breast and, using both hands, breaks it in half. Then, using two fingers with his pinkie delicately extended, he inserts the entire half chicken breast into his mouth. As he chews the chicken, bones and all, it sounds like someone just turned on a garbage disposal full of marbles. Then slowly, ever so slowly, small bones start to appear through his mustache. When he finishes with a chicken bone, there is not enough meat left on it to attract a starving ant.

Watching him drink is probably more fun than

watching him eat. He drinks only boilermakers — whiskey with a beer chaser.

Bubba, however, takes boilermakers to new heights. His version is a large glass of Lord Calvert and Coke, followed by a large glass of beer with ice cubes in it. It's a disgusting sight, but Bubba has dedicated his life to Lord Calvert and friends.

One day, Bubba invited me to lunch. Someone had told him about a new cafe that served country-style food. It was a typical country cookin' place, a small house that had been converted to a restaurant. The tablecloths were red checkered. The menu was a large blackboard hanging on the wall. It listed four meats and twelve vegetables. The waitress took my order first — country fried steak, black-eyed peas and turnip greens.

While I was ordering, Bubba was studying the menu like the waitress was going to give him a pop quiz. She said, "What can I get for you, sir?"

"I think I'll have the country fried steak and a side order of chicken," he answered.

Confused, the waitress said, "A side order of chicken?"

Bubba said, "Sure. I'll pay the full price, just bring me a side order of chicken."

"You must be extra hungry today," I said.

"No, I've just always thought that country fried steak and chicken go real good together."

The waitress said, "And what vegetable would you like, sir?"

Without missing a beat, Bubba said, "All of them."

It was a sight to behold. There sat my friend Bubba eating two meats and twelve vegetables. It was a little embarrassing when the employees in the kitchen started to peer out at Bubba. They seemed to take a good deal of interest in the chicken-bones-out-of-the-mustache trick.

We had finished our meal and were sitting there having a cup of coffee when two young men came in and sat down across the room from us. It was apparent from their dress that they were construction workers on their lunch hour. One of them had long, stringy blond hair that came down to his shoulders. When Bubba noticed the long hair, he turned to me and in a loud voice said, "Boy! You never have a Weedeater when you need one, do you?"

"Well, Bubba," I said, "this is another place I can never come back to."

I have never been able to figure out exactly what kind of a character flaw I have that makes me want to hang out with this mountain of a man. It seems that every time we are together, he either says or does something to embarrass me.

A few years ago, we were in New Orleans. It was New Year's Eve and the French Quarter was packed with celebrating tourists. Bubba had consumed more than his usual number of boilermakers, and as we say down south, he was "feelin' no pain."

Near the end of the last block of the French Quarter, there was a group of folks holding signs with religious slogans written on them. I thought we were going to get past them without being accosted, but one of the men carrying a sign that said "Repent or burn in Hell" stopped Bubba and said, "Sir, do you know that Jesus Christ died for your sins?"

Bubba stood there for a few seconds and then, with a big loving smile on his face, said, "Son of a bitch! That was sure a nice thing for him to do."

I haven't been back to the French Quarter since. I don't think I would ever run into that man again, but it would just be too big a chance to take.

Bubba was a native of south Louisiana and was Cajun to the bottom of his chubby soul. He was beyond a shadow of a doubt the best Cajun cook in the world. He carried his own pots and pans in the trunk of his car and would cook a giant Cajun dinner for anybody who would ask him.

One of the great joys of his life was to come to my house and cook one of his specialties for the family. His hospitality, however, was not without its costs.

Bubba started cooking by melting two sticks of butter. No matter what he was cooking, he needed enough melted butter to grease a freight train. His butter use was not limited to the food. Before he was finished, every square inch of the kitchen had butter or grease on it. The cupboard handles were greasy, all of the counter tops were sticky, and even the cooking utensils felt greasy. On one occasion, we had to wash the cat.

Neatness was not one of Bubba's long suits, but the meal always made up for the hours of cleaning and scrubbing that were to follow. His red beans and rice were straight from heaven, and no human being ever made gumbo in the same league with my friend Bubba.

When the Cajun cooking craze came into vogue, he decided to go into the catering business. I knew it was a bad idea from the git go. True, he was about the best Cajun cook around, but he was also about as organized as a billy goat. His plan was to go to people's homes for wedding receptions, important dinners or almost any occasion, and prepare a wonderful dinner on the premises.

He only had three jobs.

On the first, everything went well and he made a pocketful of money. He was so pleased that he was talking about expanding and maybe even advertising on TV.

The second job did not go quite as well. Midway through the dinner, he ran out of sterno. The food on the buffet was getting cold, so Bubba filled the sterno cans with lighter fluid. During the ensuing explosion, the hostess caught fire. Her dress was ruined, but fortunately she was unhurt. As a matter of fact, she felt well enough to try and kill Bubba with a sterling silver soup ladle.

The third job was a short one. They never even got to dinner, because Bubba set fire to the kitchen and the entire house burned to the ground in a matter of minutes. Bubba was melting butter on all four burners when the fire broke out.

The last letter I got from Bubba, he was working at a nuclear power plant just outside Savannah.

God help us.

Professional Gossip

Gossip can be an ugly thing. It has ruined lives, toppled empires, and spoiled marriages. Gossip, however, can be fun if it's handled by experts.

We had two such experts in my hometown, Miss Lucille and Miss Emma. These two ladies had devoted a lifetime to polishing their gossip skills and countless years sharpening their tongues to a razor-like sharpness. They held their sessions on Miss Emma's screened-in front porch. Both ladies were doing needlepoint while seated in large, white rocking chairs. There were no rules once the gossip started. They would say anything about anybody. It was free-style, take-no-prisoners gossip. It usually sounded something like this:

"Poor old Mrs. Ross . . . those kids of hers are driving her to an early grave."

"Ain't that the truth. Just goes to show, they're more trouble and heartaches when they're grown than they were as babies."

"What's Charles doing?"

"Lord only knows. He ain't drawed three sober breaths in a row since he got back from the Army."

"Does he work?"

"Lord God knows, you cain't work if you're too drunk to stand up. He was a house painter for a while, but got fired when his boss found the liquor he hid in the commode tank. His wife left him, you know. Poor thing . . . I guess she just couldn't take no more."

"Where is he now?"

"Lord only knows. Last thing I heard, he was down in Macon laid up with a woman. It's a wonder his mama ain't slap gray headed with worry."

"Have you met the new preacher?"

"Not only that, I met his bottle blonde wife."

"Does she bleach her hair?"

"You just look at those black roots and make up your own mind?"

"Did you like her?"

"Oh, she's all right, but she don't act much like a preacher's wife. You know what I think? I think if she had the chance, she'd gossip."

"You don't mean it, not the preacher's wife."

"I sure do mean it."

"If there's one thing on God's earth I can't stand, it's a gossip."

"Ain't that the Lord's truth."

"Did you hear about Ruth Whitlock leaving her husband?"

Memorable
Punch Lines

I guess there is no subject on earth that somebody hasn't made up a joke about. There are clean jokes, dirty jokes, long ones, short ones, physical ones and mental ones. Jokes are different as a rule, but they all have one thing in common — a punch line.

If it is a good punch line, the joke is funny. If it is a bad punch line, the joke falls flat. If the joke has no punch line, then it was probably told by Milton Berle.

I have long felt that punch lines by themselves are funny. If the punch line is good enough, you don't even need to know the joke. When you hear a good punch line, only two things can happen: Either you laugh because it is funny even without the joke, or the punch line reminds you of the joke and you still laugh.

I have been collecting punch lines for years, and I think I have the ten best punch lines of all time. See if you agree, or perhaps you can add to the list:

1. He'll bite you.
2. Hey Lady! Your sign fell down.
3. Wadda ya think this is, a duck?
4. The one in the middle is definitely Willie Nelson.
5. No wonder you're cold, you kicked all your dirt off.
6. Your sister Rose is dead.
7. I hope it didn't spoil your weekend.
8. The regiment votes to repair it.
9. Come on, wise guy, we're going to the sergeant.
10. It's not yo cheese.

I guess everybody likes a good joke, but a good punch line is something for the ages.

The Ballad Of Boney And Claude

I went to high school with a lot of out-and-out characters. My class reunions are always something to behold. The real fun of a class reunion is discovering how everybody turns out.

The treasurer of our senior class was an old girl named Ima Jean Bailey. She was about five-foot-ten, and after a big meal she weighed about ninety pounds. She was so skinny that she could get into a T-shirt from either end. We all had nicknames in high school, and poor old skinny Ima Jean became known to one and all as "Boney." It didn't take long before even the teachers were calling her "Boney." She never openly admitted it, but I always thought she took some pride in her nickname. She was a bright girl with a lot of personality and everybody in school knew and liked her.

The captain of our football team was our fullback, Claude Williams. He was a mountain of a lad, about six-foot-three inches tall and weighed 265. Claude was older than the rest of us because he had failed three years on his way to being a senior in high school. The standard joke was that Claude was the only student in our school who could vote. Claude didn't seem to mind the joke. It was not that he was good natured, it was just that he didn't understand it. Claude would play football and that was about it. He was the only person I ever knew who failed music appreciation. The point I'm trying to make is that, above all else, Claude was dumb. Nice, but dumb.

Midway through our senior year, Ima Jean and Claude fell madly, passionately in love. And thus began "the ballad of Boney and Claude."

Shortly after we graduated, Claude joined the Army. He was discharged three years later with one stripe and a tattoo that said "Ima Jean" under a red rose.

Claude went to plumber's school on the G.I. Bill. The day he graduated, Boney and Claude were married. He was thirty minutes late getting to his own wedding; seems he couldn't remember which church to go to. When the minister asked Claude, "Do you take this woman to be your lawfully wedded wife?" Claude said, "Yeah." There was low laughter in the church, but as soon as Boney punched him in the ribs with her elbow, he said, "Boy! Howdy, I sure do."

As we left the church, we were all sure that they would live happily ever after. It was more than obvious that they were very much in love. You could see it in her eyes, and I don't guess you have a girl's name tattooed on your arm if you don't really love her.

The years were not kind to the love birds. Claude bounced from one job to another. He was a hard, willing worker, but since he had the IQ of a lug wrench, it was very hard for him to hold a job for very long.

One night, while they were watching an "Iron-sides" rerun on their rented TV, Boney said, "Claude, I think I have figured out a way that we can get out of debt."

In his usual alert manner, Claude said, "Huh?"

Boney told him that they were going to rob a bank.

Claude said, "What if we get caught?"

Boney explained that if they went to a small country bank and waited until it was almost empty of customers, there would be little or no risk.

"We ain't even got a gun and no money to buy one," Claude said.

"We don't need a real gun. I saw a water pistol in the dime store the other day, and it looks exactly like a .45 automatic. Nobody on earth can tell it from a real gun."

Claude said, "Yeah, and if somebody tries to stop us, we'll drown 'em."

"Don't worry, Honey," Boney said, "I'll explain exactly how to do it."

The next day, they went to the dime store and bought the water pistol. Claude played with the gun while Boney checked the map for a small town that had a bank. When they found just the right size town, they drove there in Claude's pick-up to check it out. Everything seemed perfect. The town was so small it only had one policeman. It also held the one and only branch of the Farmers and Merchants Bank of Ritter County.

Boney and Claude watched the bank all that day. There was only one teller and the manager. Most of the time there were no customers at all. Boney made a mental note. The manager went to lunch at twelve o'clock, leaving the elderly woman teller alone in the bank. It seemed like the perfect bank for two trainee robbers to start with.

That night, Boney wrote a note that said, "Put all your money in this sack and nobody will get hurt." She then made Claude put down his comic book while she explained to him what his job would be the next day. She spoke slowly and gave detailed instructions.

"Claude, here is all you have to do. We wait until the manager goes to lunch and the teller is alone. I'll wait in the truck with the motor running. All you have to do, Claude, is go into the bank, hand the lady the note and the sack and show her the gun. She will fill the sack full of money, and you walk out of the bank very calmly, and then we drive off. Believe me, Claude," she went on, "nothing can go wrong if you do exactly as I tell you. This is foolproof."

Claude smiled and said, "It'll be like takin' candy away from someone fallin' off a log."

The next day they got up and dressed. Boney went over the plan three more times to make sure Claude had it clearly in mind. They stopped on the way out of town and filled the pick-up with gas. The sun was shining and it seemed like a perfect day to "go into business for yourself," as Boney said.

They got to the front of the bank right on time. It was five minutes till twelve, and there were no customers in the bank. The noon news came on the truck radio, and right on cue, the manager walked out of the bank, got in his car and drove away.

Boney said, "O.K., Claude, do you have the note?"

"Yep!"

"Do you have the sack?"

"Yep!"

"Do you have the gun?"

"Yep!"

"Do you remember what to do?"

Claude said, "Dawg gone, Boney, sometimes you treat me like I ain't got no sense at all. Don't you remember I graduated twelfth in my class from plumbing school?"

Boney said, "Claude, you ain't going in there to unstop a commode, you're going in there to rob 'em. Besides, there were only ten people in your class."

They kissed and Claude got out of the truck and strolled into the bank. He walked up to the teller's window, as cool as the center seed of a cucumber. The elderly lady smiled and said, "Can I help you, young man?"

Claude smiled back and said, "Yes, ma'am. I got a note here for you from my wife."

She read the note and said, "You wouldn't want to shoot me, now would you, my boy?"

Claude paused and said, "I wouldn't mind." She started to fill the sack with loose bills.

Outside, Boney's heart nearly stopped when the town's only police car pulled up beside her, stopped and the policeman got out and walked into the bank. Claude did not see him come in.

The officer sized up the situation immediately. In a loud, commanding voice, he said, "What's going on here?" With no hesitation at all, Claude spun around and squirted the policeman right between the eyes with his water pistol.

Boney and Claude were not at our last class reunion, but I bet their ears were burning.

Wit & Wisdom From Ludlow

❝ The country started going to hell when children stopped licking the dasher. ❞

*

❝ The secret to a happy marriage is for the husband and wife to grow up without growing apart. ❞

*

❝ We should all smile more, because sunshine is good for your teeth. ❞

My Dixie, Forever

In the past few years, the song "Dixie" has come under great fire from folks who say it is racist and conjures up images of segregation. It has reached the point where it is almost rare to hear it played in public anymore.

I can only speak for myself, of course, but I freely admit that when I hear "Dixie" played, it does, indeed, conjure up certain images.

"Dixie" makes me think of live oak trees, the Indian River, and the Atlanta Cracker baseball team. It makes me think of cornbread, Coca-Cola, and dawn in Laurel, Mississippi. It makes me think of Dublin, Georgia, and the wonderful people there who celebrate St. Patrick's Day for two weeks.

"Dixie" makes me think of gospel music, Brother Dave, and Daytona Beach. It makes me think of Minnie Pearl, dove hunting, and children who say "Yes, ma'am" and "No, ma'am." It makes me think of tailgating before a football game and the warm feeling you get when your team wins.

"Dixie" makes me think of Knoxville, meat skins, and the smell of honeysuckle. It makes me think of Peachtree Street in the rain, the Varsity, and stopping at Stuckey's. It makes me think of the Grand Old Opry, the Catfish Festival, and five hundred acres of snow-white cotton.

It makes me think of front porches, rocking chairs, and cold lemonade. It makes me think of barbecue, Brunswick stew, and the smell of hickory burning. It makes me think of Jefferson, Jackson, and Jimmy Carter. It makes me think of the French Quarter, Spanish moss, and Jack Daniels.

"Dixie" makes me think of Madison, Georgia; Decatur, Alabama; and the Florida Panhandle. It makes me think of Louis Armstrong, home-grown tomatoes, and the Masters. It makes me think of those wonderful folks who live, love, work and die there.

It brings back memories whenever I hear it. Good memories. I get giant goose bumps when I hear the first six notes. I consider it a great gift from the Almighty to be allowed to "live and die in Dixie."

I don't expect everyone to feel the same way about this old song that I do, but I do wish they would try and understand that it's not about the Civil War; it's about today, tomorrow, and, hopefully, about forever.

I don't mind if you don't like it, but please, don't get your nose out of joint because I do.

The Man Who Invented Sex

We have a great many holidays in this country, and let the record clearly show that I love
every one of them. I am usually the first person
to leave work on a holiday and the last to return.
I take my holidays seriously.

There is something, however, that is laying
heavy on my heart. It saddens me greatly to realize that in no country in the world do we honor
the inventor of sex with a holiday. I think it's
probably more an oversight of ignorance than of
design. Therefore, allow me to educate you about
this great event.

Sex was discovered in 1936 by a Swedish sailor
on shore leave in Jacksonville, Florida. His name
was Lars Sex. He went back to his ship and told
his friends of his discovery and, as they say, "The
rest is history."

Lars retired (from the Navy, not from experi-
mentation) to his native Sweden and passed
away in relative obscurity in 1959.

The world owes this great man more than we
can ever repay. Yet, he is in no history book, and

there is no holiday honoring his name. It was only recently that he was even mentioned in polite conversation.

There is, however, a discreet group of people worldwide that pays special tribute to Lars. I understand that at this very writing, millions and millions of private celebrations are going on in every imaginable place, from the back seat of a 1957 Chevy to the New York sewer system.

Lars Sex . . . hallowed be his name.

Say It All, But Keep It Short

You can go into every souvenir shop from just south of the Mason-Dixon Line to Key West, and you will find that they all have one thing in common: They all have at least one so-called "Southern Dictionary."

You know the ones I'm talkin' about. They give you a word and then tell you what it means in the south. Example:

> Cheer = Something you sit in,
>   as in "rocking cheer."
> Jeet = Have you eaten?

There must be ten thousand of these books on the market, and I have never found one even mildly amusing. I'm not offended by them, I just think they're boring. I have never felt that the way Southerners pronounce words is what a southern accent is all about, although it is certainly a big part of it. I think it is the word pictures southern people paint that make us more fun to listen to.

If we want to explain how mean someone is, we might say any of the following:

1. He is so mean, he would knock you naked and hide your clothes.
2. He is mean enough to push little ducks in the water.
3. He's so mean he would pull up little corn.
4. He'll knock the tar out of you.
5. He'll stomp a mud hole in you, then walk it dry.
6. He'll hit your ass in the head with a rock.
7. She hit him so hard, his shirt tail went up his back like a window shade.
8. He could hunt bears with a switch.

In the South, it is not enough to say someone is ugly. We say:

1. She is so ugly she has to sneak up on a glass of water.
2. She's ugly enough to knock a buzzard off a gut wagon.
3. He's ugly enough to make a freight train take a dirt road.
4. He looked like his face caught on fire and somebody beat it out with a shovel.
5. The whole family was so ugly that, when they made home movies, they hired stand-ins.
6. She was beaten with an ugly stick.
7. That child was so ugly that his mama had to hang a pork chop around his neck to get the dogs to play with him.

8. Ugly enough to gag a maggot.

One of the worst things you can be in the South is lazy. There are a lot of synonyms for lazy, like sorry, shiftless, no account, and useless. There are also many descriptive phrases used to cover this unfortunate condition:

1. He is as sorry as gully dirt.
2. He ain't nothin' but a "layabout."
3. That's one old dog that won't hunt.
4. He's too sorry to kill.
5. He wouldn't scratch if he had a four-pound flea.
6. He's so lazy he gets somebody else to call his dogs.
7. He was born lazy and had a relapse.
8. He was born tired and raised lazy.

For some reason that I have never quite understood, people in the South take great pride in coming from small towns. The smaller the town, the more pride they seem to take. They also find great descriptive phrases to tell just how small their home town was:

1. My home town was so small that the town prostitute was a virgin.
2. The head of the Mafia was Japanese.
3. My home town was so small that both city limit signs were on the same post.
4. The city hall was so small that it had humpback mice.

5. I went there to make a speech to the Rotary Club, but the guy couldn't get off work.

Hard drinking men are almost a way of life in the South, and as with all hard-drinking men, sooner or later John Barleycorn robs them of their common sense and they wind up being described as:

1. Loop legged drunk
2. Knee walkin' drunk
3. Commode huggin' drunk
4. Too drunk to sing
5. Drunker than a three-eyed goat
6. Face down in the gully
7. Drunker than Cooter Johnson
8. He took bad drunk

In order to truly understand Southerners, you must listen closely, because we take great pride in our descriptive words and phrases. The following will probably come under miscellaneous Southern words and phrases:

In the rural south, a semi is referred to as a transfer truck. An automobile accelerator is the foot feed. A woman never just divorces her husband, she quits him or gets shed of him. A woman never has a tantrum, she has a "fit," or, in extreme cases, a "hissy fit." We never start a car, we crank it.

There are two kinds of children, lap children and yard children. A grandfather never asks a grandchild for a kiss, he asks for a little sugar. A husband never tells his wife she is a good cook. He will say, "Honey, you're the best cook I ever ate behind." If you're not considering something, you "ain't studyin' it." You never open a car window, you "crack the window."

If a man is repeatedly unfaithful to his wife, his neighbors will say, "He's a right hard dog to keep under the porch."

If your meal was good, you should tell your wife that it was so good that your tongue almost slapped your brains out. If a country road was not very straight, it was said to be "crooked as a dog's hind leg." If it was straight, it was said to be so straight that you could drive it drunk.

When you leave a friend's house after a visit, he will say one of several things, like: "Come back;" "Don't be gone so long;" "Hold it in the road;" or, "Keep it between the ditches."

When you first see somebody, the standard Southern greeting is, "Hey," or, "How's your mama 'n 'em?" You never order just milk in a restaurant; you must tell them the kind you prefer, as in sweet milk, chocolate milk, or buttermilk. The same holds true with bread. Generally speaking, only four kinds of bread are eaten in the South: rolls, cornbread, biscuits, and loafbread, the latter being any type of presliced bread that is bought at a store. If one is hungry, he might say that he is so hungry he has the "weak trembles," or, "I'm so hungry my stomach thinks my throat has been cut."

If a Southern lady is thirsty, she would say that she is "about to perish." If that same Southern lady feels faint, she "has the vapors." If a woman in the South is referred to as low, it has nothing to do with her character; it refers to her height, as in, "She's a little bitty low woman." It might be said of a short man that, "He is so short he could sit on the ground and dangle his feet."

If someone has been sick but is recovering, we might say that he did feel poorly but now is feeling tolerable. If a Southerner is sore from a fall or too much exercise, he is "stove up." If a child does not have good color, he is said to be "bilious."

If one is tired, they are "bout past goin'." It would seem that nobody ever dies in the South; they expire, or pass away, or cross over, and sometimes they are "called home." Strangely enough, there are no toilets in the South; there are bathrooms, restrooms, powder rooms, as well as little boys' and little girls' rooms.

If a fruit or vegetable at the store is not of the highest quality, it is said to be "no account," or, "It ain't fit to eat," or, "Not fit for hogs." If a man had a stormy and active love life, people would say, "He sowed so many wild oats that he's up for a federal farm grant."

I'm just sure that for our new friends, we must be a source of great confusion. I'm also sure that once we get past the language barrier, they like us and we like them.

I was reading a story in the local newspaper a few weeks ago. It seems that a legislator in

California had introduced a bill to make English the official language of California. I had to smile as I read it, because if they ever introduced a bill like that in the South, we'd all be in a hell of a shape.

White Trash Guidelines

When you do humor for a living, the very first thing you learn is that most groups, ethnic or otherwise, are overly sensitive. It is almost impossible to tell a joke to a live audience without offending someone. The only exception may be that very large group known as the white trash of the world.

In my many years as a talk show host, I have never had anyone call my boss and say, "I'm white trash, and Ludlow is making fun of us on the air." I'm not gullible enough to think that they don't mind white trash jokes. I can only assume, therefore, that they don't know they're white trash.

Let us examine, then, some of the qualifications one must have to belong to this somewhat less than select group.

The first myth we must dispose of is that being white trash is somehow related to your income. Nothing could be further from the truth. I once knew a vice-president of a bank. He was rich, drove a big car, and was the Sunday school director at his church. It turned out that he was also three things that nobody ever suspected; he was an embezzler, he was fooling around with the church organist, and he was white trash.

The United States Congressmen who were caught in Abscam were not only gravy suckin' pigs, but in every case they were white trash. Consider the following facts about white trash and you'll see what I mean.

1. A recent survey has shown that white trash makes up 87.9 percent of the U.S. toothpick market.

2. White trash prefers to use their front porches to store their discarded kitchen appliances.

3. The first three words that white trash children learn to say are, "Mama," "Daddy," and "shit," not necessarily in that order.

4. White trash considers abandoned cars to be an important part of their landscape architecture.

5. White trash children must start smoking by age twelve.

6. White trash considers chickens to be household pets.

7. White trash are taught from infancy how to speak with their mouth full of food and, at the same time, gesture with whatever eating utensil may be handy at the moment.

8. White trash park only in handicapped parking spaces.

9. White trash are the exclusive market for white-sidewall-tire planters.

10. While all white trash men are not wife beaters, all wife beaters are white trash.

11. The code of the white trash requires that any of them attending a sporting event must be intoxicated prior to the end of the National Anthem.

12. Approximately seventy-eight percent of white trash have been fingerprinted by their seventeenth birthday.

13. White trash must have at least one relative named for an animal: Buck, Snake, Weasel, etc.

14. While there are some exceptions, generally speaking, white trash will not marry blood relatives closer than nephews.

15. White trash do not change their babies' diapers on any day with a "U" in it.

16. White trash are generally kind to their dogs. They usually provide a large oil spill for them to lie in.

17. The favorite mode of travel for white trash is any vehicle with not more than three fenders.

18. White trash considers man's best friend not to be the dog, but the jumper cable.

19. At least one member of a white trash family must have the surname "Junior."

20. White trash, by nature, have strange senses of humor. They think any joke about a bathroom or a body function is funny.

21. White trash men all refer to their wives as "my old lady."

22. The cars of white trash will not run without some fuzzy object hanging from the rearview mirror.

23. The white trash community cannot under-stand why a professional wrestler has never been appointed to the Supreme Court.

24. White trash consider any pickup with lawn furniture in the back to be a limo.

25. When white trash tell you that they are self-educated, it means they read the *National Enquirer* every week.

I don't want to leave the wrong impression about white trash. They are not all bad. As a matter of fact, over the years many of them have risen to great heights. They have become gen-erals, presidents, and dictators of many coun-tries. At least two of them have appeared in the famous Robert L. Ripley's *Believe It or Not* — one of them for being an only child, and the other for having liability insurance on his car.

The Ultimate Barbecue Joint

I hope, by now, that most people realize I am one of the world's foremost authorities on barbecue. Goodness knows, I've told them enough times. I have eaten good "Q" all over the south. I've eaten it in Mom & Pop joints and in the big franchised places.

One time, when I was desperate, I even ate beef barbecue.

After all these years of testing, re-testing, learning and experimenting, I have decided to take the big plunge and open up the world's first perfect barbecue joint.

A barbecue joint is much more than just good barbecue. There are actually dozens of elements that go into the "perfect" place.

In my travels in rural north Georgia, I have discovered the perfect, and I mean the *perfect*, location. On a recent Sunday outing with the family, we found an old vacant, red brick church. It's not big, but it's big enough. It still has the stained glass windows and it will give me just the right atmosphere for my barbecue joint. It goes without saying, of course, that the name is important. The name of my place will be "The Que, Stew and Pew."

The menu will be simple but will satisfy the tastes of any true southern barbecue lover:

1. We will serve pork only. Research clearly shows that people who eat beef barbecue also like tongue, liver, broccoli, and carry pictures of commies in their wallets. The pork would be either sliced or chopped, since we are trying to please the masses.

2. Our Brunswick stew will be made in a gigantic black pot, and it will be stirred from time to time with a sawed-off canoe paddle. It will contain only the wonderful things that the good Lord decreed should go into real Brunswick Stew. That means no English peas.

3. We will serve white loaf bread. Our bread will be the freshest available anywhere. We will serve it fresh from the sack or toasted over the same grill that the meat was cooked on.

4. Our fourth and final food item will be potato chips. Not the kind with ridges, not the kind that is flavored with garlic, or onion, or barbecue, just plain old honest-to-goodness fresh, wonderful potato chips.

These will be the only food items sold. If somebody comes in and wants a cheeseburger, we will direct him to the nearest drive-in window at the Burger Doodle.

If someone comes in and wants barbecue beef, the waitresses will all laugh and the cook will holler things about his Mama until he leaves.

Like the food menu, the drink menu will be simple, yet elegant. We will serve sweet iced tea in large, large glasses. This will be brought to your table by the waitress. If a customer does not want iced tea, we will offer soft drinks. They, however, will not be brought to your table. They will be self-service and kept in a large drink box full of ice cold water. The soft drinks, of course, will be in bottles only; to serve one in a can would seriously affect the type of atmosphere that we are trying to create. We will serve Coca-Cola, Pepsi, R.C. Cola, and both orange and grape Nehi.

In a true southern barbecue joint, the employees are very important. We will have three waitresses: Roxy, Dixie and Jolean.

The cashier will double as the cook during the rush hours. His name will be Eugene Lamar, and he will keep a kitchen match dangling from the corner of his mouth at all times. If we cannot hire someone named Eugene Lamar, then we will hire someone with initials for a first name like J.W. or W.D.

The Stew, Que and Pew will be open only on Friday, Saturday, and Sunday. I will need the other four days to make bank deposits and get ready for the weekend rush. I will put an ad in the paper as soon as I open, so you can come to the world's only perfect barbecue joint.

In the meantime, if you run into anybody named Eugene Lamar, would you ask him to call me?

Old And Dear Friends

I guess it comes as no news to anyone, the pain of losing an old friend. Sure, we all realize that time marches on and that none of us is going to live forever. But that doesn't make the loss of a friend or loved one any easier to cope with.

In the last few years, I seem to be losing old friends in big bunches. It was bad enough when Edgar Bergen died, but the same day that we lost Edgar Bergen, we also lost Charlie McCarthy and Mortimer Snerd.

When Al Capp passed away, think of the friends that went with him: Li'l Abner, Daisy Mae, Mammie and Pappy Yocum, Earthquake McGoon, the Scraggs, and, of course, the inside man at the Skonkworks, Big Barnsmell.

When Walt Kelley died, so did Pogo and all our wonderful friends from the Okeefeenokee.

I guess the only thing that keeps me going in the face of such losses is the knowledge that the angels must have really rejoiced when they saw those folks coming.

The General Store

Convenience stores are wonderful. In the last few years, they have sprung up on street corners all over America. Their presence allows us to get the things we need twenty-four hours a day, seven days a week. You can stop on the way home from work and pick up anything you need, from a tank of gas to a dozen hot dog buns.

You can buy antifreeze at two o'clock in the morning or send your brother-in-law a money order on Sunday. When the late show is over and you develop a sweet tooth, that wonderful Twinkie is waiting for you, just seconds away. Not only is it waiting, but so is the half gallon of chocolate milk that you can't live without. Let the record clearly show that without our convenience stores, our lives would not be nearly as pleasant as they are today.

However, as wonderful as they are, they are at least partially responsible for the loss of another part of Americana. I refer, of course, to the general store.

You could find them in every small town in

America. They were the center of trade and commerce at most country crossroads. They were all the same, and yet all were different.

The general store that is locked in my memory was a wooden building with two gas pumps under a wooden carport-type drive through. One pump was marked "Regular" and the other proudly said "Ethyl." The front of the store had a wooden bench under one of the two large dirty windows. There was a double door with a double screen door. On the screen of each door were blue and yellow letters that said, "Colonial Is Good Bread."

Just to the left of the front door was a hand-cranked kerosene dispenser that clearly showed years of spills, and years of road dust was clinging to the sticky spilled kerosene. On the side of the store painted in huge letters, a sign said, "Drink Red Rock Cola." Near the very top of the screen door just over the "Colonial Is Good Bread" sign hung a huge ball of cotton. It was widely believed, in those days, that flies thought the cotton was a large moth and therefore would not enter the store.

Once inside the store, it was a surprise to see not only how big it was, but also the great variety of things that were offered for sale. There was an older man behind the long wooden counter. He would look up as you entered and say, without smiling, "Come in the house."

You would say, "How ya doin'?"

He'd answer, "Never been better, or had less." He would then pause and say, "Can I hep ya?"

"No, just lookin' around, thanks."

The wall on the left was full of shelves from floor to ceiling. The lower shelves had canned goods and the top shelf held the toilet tissue. Hanging on one of the shelves was a cut-off broom stick with a nail in the end. It was used to knock the toilet paper off the high shelf. On the bottom shelf were boxes of Kotex. You could not tell what was in the boxes because every box was wrapped neatly in plain brown paper.

Also along the wall was a red drink box that said "Coca-Cola, the pause that refreshes." When you opened the door on top of the drink box, you could see only dark water with a large chunk of ice floating around.

You thrust your hand into the water. It is so cold you think your finger nails are going to drop off. Hurrying now, because of the cold, you pull out a bottle. It's an RC and you wanted a Coke. Try again. This time it's a Pepsi. On the fourth try, you come up with a Nu-Grape and decide that's close enough.

There is a built-in bottle opener on the front of the box. The container for the bottle caps is full, so your Nu-Grape cap falls to the floor. You reach for it and the man behind the counter says, "Don't worry about it, the sweeper will get it."

The back of the store is split, half for the butcher and half for the feed. The chicken feed is in ten, fifteen and twenty-five-pound sacks. The sacks have beautiful flower designs in every shade of the rainbow. The most popular designs seem to be small flowers. In those days, "pretty feed sacks" were much in demand to make clothes with. There were not many boys or girls living in the South at that time who had not worn at least one feed sack shirt or blouse.

The meat department consists of a large display cooler made of white porcelain. The front is all glass so you can see what is available that day. There is a scale on top of the cooler and fly paper hangs from the ceiling. The floor behind the porcelain cooler is covered with sawdust.

The long, U-shaped counter in the middle of the store was full of displays. One is a rack full of pipes. The sign reads, "Buy two cans of Prince Albert smoking tobacco and get a genuine briar pipe, FREE." Another display has a sign with a picture of a man in a white smock with a stethoscope hanging from his neck. The caption under the picture says, "Doctors prefer Camel cigarettes, three to one."

Near the large brass cash register lies a punch board and a sign that says, "Punch out the star and win a single shot .22 rifle...only ten cents a chance." To the left of the punch board is a large hoop of cheese under a glass cover. There is a small barrel of cookies, a pyramid of Tube Rose snuff cans and a ten-inch by twelve-inch glass display case full of case pocket knives.

The whole store had a personality of its own. It was old, it was disorganized and it was dusty, but it was part of my childhood and part of the south.

Yes, I love the modern convenience stores, but I wish, just one more time, I could hear that old man say, "Come in the house."

The Flab Fight

I'm one of those folks who continues to engage in the flab fight. In my lifetime, I have been on just about any kind of diet that anyone would suggest to me. I have been successful on some; others I have stayed on for less than twenty minutes. I have lost, at one time or another, about two thousand pounds, and by doing so, I know the thrill of victory. Unfortunately, I have gained back about 2,050 pounds, making me an expert on the agony of deflab.

I have been a member of Weight Watchers, European Health Spa, and even thought about becoming a moonie (I have never seen a fat moonie). I have tried a total fast, a partial fast, and a not-so-fast fast.

It has occurred to me that I can perform a great public service if I share my failures with my readers. Who knows? Somebody out there may be getting ready to try something that has already failed for me, and perhaps, just perhaps, I can help others stay away from some of the useless diets I have tried.

THE BRAZIL DIET
You can have one South American a day, and all the kumquats you want.

THE ALCATRAZ POTATO DIET
You are locked in a cell, and three times a day a man comes by and shows you a picture of a bowl of mashed potatoes.

THE ELEPHANT DIET
You can have one elephant a week, cooked any way you want it. However, you must personally kill the elephant with a butter knife.

THE OLYMPIC DIET
You can have one full meal every four years.

THE JIM AND TAMMY FAYE DIET
You don't get much to eat on this diet, and it makes you pray and cry a lot.

THE C.I.A. DIET
I understand this is a wonderful diet, but nobody will give me the details.

People who enjoy good food are always going to be faced with dieting. The only hope I can give you is there are probably more old fat people than there are old doctors.

Unanswered Questions

Life, in general, is a puzzle to most people. Once we identify a problem, it is human nature to seek out a solution. When there is no apparent solution, you can spend long hours wondering about them. I've made a list of some of the things I wonder about:

1. Why are all men named Al called Big Al? Never mind if he is five-foot-two and weighs 125 pounds. If his name is Al, sooner or later he will be referred to as Big Al.

2. Mickey Mouse is obviously black. Why, then, was he not more involved in the civil rights movement?

3. Why do they call gay people "gay"? If there is a reason for it, I've never been able to find out.

4. Why do gas stations lock their bathrooms? Are they afraid someone is going to steal something? If so, what?

5. Why do only skinny people drink diet drinks? Think about it; have you ever seen a fat man drinking a Tab or a Diet Pepsi?

6. Why do rich people give their children cutesy nicknames like Bucky or Buffy? Looking back, I don't think I ever knew a rich person called Spike, Pig or Spit.

There are probably no answers to any of these questions, but that doesn't stop me from wondering.

Wit & Wisdom From Ludlow

❝If there is, indeed, more than one way to skin a cat, I don't want to know about it.❞

＊

❝A good education is very important. It's the only way you can be sure of getting a job in the shade.❞

＊

❝He was so cheap, he wouldn't pay ten cents to see Jimmy Hoffa ride a bicycle through a two-inch pipe.❞

The Perfect Saturday

Growing up is not all its cracked up to be. When the pages of the calendar start dropping off at their frantic pace, and those seven precious teen years are behind us, there is a gradual changing of values. The new set of values is neither better nor worse, just different. Use of leisure time is a perfect example.

My idea of a perfect Saturday now is a quiet day of rest at home, a little TV and dinner out with my lovely wife and best friend Diane.

Only a few years ago, however, this would have bored the pants off me. In those pre-teen years, my perfect Saturday would have started at noon at the B&F grill. The B&F was located next door to my favorite place in the whole world, the East Point Theatre. We didn't call it a theatre in those days. It was simply called "the show," as in, "Let's go to the show."

After a B&F hamburger and a small Coke, I would go outside and get in line. The show opened at one o'clock, and on Saturday there was always a line. Once you had paid your nine cents admission, the next move was to get your popcorn and Walnettos (if you had a dime) and move to the very first row. The show didn't start until 1:15, so you had to sit there and wait. It seemed to be hours before the big curtain opened.

The first thing shown was always the previews. They showed everything that would be on the following week. When the previews were over, the newsreel came on. Several companies made newsreels: Pathe, Movietone and Fox are three that I remember. They all had war news, and I can remember straining to see if I could spot one of my uncles as the camera showed the troops in Europe. I never did, but I never quit trying.

After the war news, they usually had a humorous news feature about a monkey that could water ski, or a man riding a bicycle coast to coast.

The newsreel was followed by a comedy, not to be confused with a cartoon. A comedy was a fifteen-minute feature and usually starred the Three Stooges or Andy Clyde, sometimes Leon Errol or Edgar Kennedy. If you were lucky, it could even be a Joe McDoakes or a Pete Smith special.

No matter what the comedy was, it always had basically the same plot: Some poor guy would get into a lot of trouble, with either his wife, his boss or the police. The fun came in watching him bumble and stumble his way out of the mess. It was fun because you knew in advance that it was going to have a happy ending.

The comedy was followed by the first feature. It was a "B" western, although there were two kinds of "B" westerns: One starred the singing cowboys, and the other featured the action cowboys. The best known singing cowboys of my day were Gene Autry, Roy Rogers, Jimmy Wakely, Eddie Dean, Tex Ritter and Rex Allen. There were others, but these were my favorites.

The list of the action cowboys is longer, and they were more fun to watch because it was all action. No time was taken up by singing a song to a horse or to some old girl in a long dress. The list of best known action "B" movie cowboys does not include two of my idols: Randolph Scott and John Wayne. By the time I came along, both of them had graduated to the big budget westerns.

My "B" western heroes were Charles Starrett as the Durango Kid, Lash LaRue, Whip Wilson, Bob Steele, Johnny Mack Brown, Sunset Carson, Hopalong Cassidy, Bob Livingstone, Wild Bill Elliott, Alan Rocky Lane, Don (Red) Barry and Buster Crabbe.

Every good "B" cowboy had to have a sidekick, and in many cases, they stole the show. A few of the better known sidekicks were Smiley Burnette (a.k.a. Frog Millhouse), Gabby Hayes, Dub (Cannonball) Taylor, Fuzzy St. John (a.k.a. Fuzzy Q. Jones), and Max Terhune.

The hero's horse was very important, and they had wonderful names like Silver, Thunder, Topper, Rebel, White Flash and Raider.

We not only enjoyed the westerns, but I think we learned a good lesson from them. The good guy never drank, smoked or did anything that was not completely honorable. That lesson was given to us in large doses every Saturday. Good was better then evil, and when the cowboy rode into the sunset at the end of the movie, you sat there with a stomach full of popcorn and brown Walnetto stain on your face, and deep down in your heart you knew for sure that it pays to be a good guy, because good guys always win.

When the first feature was over, it was time for the serial, or, as we called it, the continued picture. There were generally twelve to sixteen chapters, and they always ended with the hero about to die in a train crash or a fire, or being eaten by a fierce jungle animal. All week long, you and your friends speculated about how the hero was going to survive. You couldn't wait to see the next chapter, especially if the hero was one of your favorite comic book characters.

Some of the better known serials were The Shadow, Batman, The Phantom (we pronounced it "The Phathumb"), The Lone Ranger, Don Winslow of the Navy, Tailspin Tommy, Captain Marvel, Zorro and The Black Commando (the black referred to his custom and not his race).

When the serial was over, it was time, at last, for the cartoon. Most of the successful cartoons have since made it big on TV. A few of my favorites were Donald Duck, Mickey Mouse, Droopy, Tom and Jerry, Daffy Duck, Silly Symphonies, Road Runner, Bugs Bunny and Porky Pig.

The cartoon usually lasted seven or eight minutes, and by the time it was over, every child in the show was on the floor with laughter.

When the last feature came on, it was regarded as the big finish. Like the "B" western we had just seen, it was always a low, low budget film. And, also like the "B" western, they were generally a series film. This feature was held for last and nobody even went to the bathroom while it was on.

Some of the better known "B" movie series were Charlie Chan, The Falcon, The Saint, The East Side Kids, The Bowery Boys, Boston Blackie, Blondie and Dagwood, Dick Tracy, The Wolfman, The Invisible Man and Joe Palooka.

There were also "B" movies that were not made in series. They had some of the all-time great stars, such as Judy Canova, Joe E. Brown, Lum and Abner, Bob Burns and The Ritz Brothers.

When the last movie was over, the entire thing started all over again. If you liked, you could stay and see it all a second time. However, as a general rule, the movie pretty well emptied out after the first show. Every child there wanted to get outside and start to play. The movie we had just seen dictated what we were going to play. If, for example, we had seen a picture with a lot of sword play, we all got our swords (usually sticks or small limbs). Garbage can lids made excellent shields.

If we had just seen a war movie, we were soon killing imaginary Germans and Japanese.

A Tarzan movie, of course, would require a rope swing.

Our wonderful Saturdays were usually brought to a close when our mothers called us in at suppertime. We were always tired, dirty and almost starving to death. When we were finally fed and cleaned, our day was almost over. But even in bed at night, with our prayers said and our eyes closed, we were still riding right alongside "Hoppy" or swimming in a quiet pond with Tarzan, Jane and Boy.

If I had a magic wand, I think my first wish would be to spend one more day on the front row.

Ten Ways To Become A Social Outcast

1. Always interrupt when other people are talking. This lets them know that what you have to say is much more important than what they are saying.

2. Whenever possible, wear your hat while eating. This will proclaim to all that you are at best a clod, and at worst, third-generation white trash.

3. Comment often on other people's physical characteristics. Short people do not know they are short and fat people do not know they are fat. They, therefore, must depend on people with no sensitivity to tell them.

4. Never say "Thank you" or "I'm sorry." It is a sign of good upbringing and you certainly don't want to be cursed with that stigma.

5. Blow your horn in traffic whenever you can. This is a rare opportunity for you to make

total strangers hate you.

6. Park in handicap parking at all times. This not only reinforces your lack of sensitivity, it also tells the world that you are too lazy to walk a few extra feet.

7. Never go to the movie to see it. Go to the movie to talk.

8. Complain to anyone who will listen. This will cause people to avoid you and will bring you the solitude that you so richly deserve.

9. Hate your job and let everyone know it. This character trait will assure you a lifetime of frustration and failure.

10. Whenever possible, be negative. Being negative will bring you undreamed of results. Not only will it make everyone around you negative, and therefore as unhappy as you are, but it will almost certainly assure you of someday being buried in an unmarked grave.

Let's Talk About It

Have you ever noticed how big the Russians are on negotiating? I always get a big laugh when I read that the Soviets have agreed to sit down at the table to negotiate with us. It reminds me of a story I heard many years ago. It goes like this:

Once upon a time, in a huge forest, a hunter and a bear suddenly found themselves face to face in a small clearing. They were both startled for a second, and then, regaining his composure, the hunter raised his gun to his shoulder. The bear said, "Wait! Let's talk about this." The hunter agreed and they sat down on the ground to begin negotiations.

"What do you want?" the bear asked.

The hunter replied, "I'm very cold. I want a fur coat. What do you want?"

"I'm very hungry," replied the bear. "The only thing I really want is a full belly."

The negotiations wore on until the hunter was so tired that he dozed off. A few minutes later, the bear got up and walked away. The hunter had his fur coat and the bear had his full belly.

That's negotiating Russian style.

The Blessed Folks

1. Blessed are those who are pleasant.
2. Blessed are those who don't have all the answers.
3. Blessed are those who laugh often.
4. Blessed are those who hug.
5. Blessed are those with a dependable bull-pen.
6. Blessed are those who get in their lane of traffic and stay there.
7. Blessed are those who serve sweet iced tea.
8. Blessed are the sportscasters who don't scream at us from our televisions.
9. Blessed are those who don't call me during my favorite TV show.
10. Blessed are those who don't pop their gum.
11. Blessed are those who know that brevity is the soul of wit.
12. Blessed are puppies.
13. Blessed are those who punt on fourth and one.

14. Blessed are those who own rocking chairs.
15. Blessed are the doctors who don't keep you waiting.
16. Blessed is the winning RBI.
17. Blessed is the gas gauge that reads "F".
18. Blessed are those who serve cornbread.
19. Blessed are seats in first class.
20. Blessed are sermons that are finished thirty minutes prior to kick-off.
21. Blessed is a baby's smile.
22. Blessed is low humidity.
23. Blessed are those who understand and love Christmas morning.

How Do You Know When It's Over?

A wise man once said, "Nothing dies harder than love, but once it's dead, it's dead forever." The thing that usually brings the most pain, however, is the fact that most people do not realize when it's over.

I therefore felt it might be a public service if I gave you some things that happen when it's really over:

1. You know it's over when she won't tell you the code for the new burglar alarm.
2. When she buys a dog and won't tell you its name.
3. When your mail starts being addressed to "Defendant."
4. When the children start to introduce you as "my ex-father."
5. When your lawyer tells you that he can't talk to you because it might be a conflict of interest.

I'm Glad Doodle Wasn't There

I have been a people watcher all my life. I think you can learn a lot by being attentive to the carrying on of your fellow human beings.

There are many places that offer excellent people watching. Las Vegas is great, with the ladies running around with their cups full of quarters. And it's hard to beat New York City, where a good part of the population seems constantly furious at their lot in life.

I am convinced, however, after a lifetime of people watching, that the best, most interesting place to do it is on airplanes and in airports.

Not long ago, I was returning from a business trip to Orlando, Florida. I was the first one on the airplane and found my seat in the first row of the smoking section. I was enjoying watching my fellow passengers board. As they passed, I could see families going home after a week at Disney World, the secretaries so proud of their fresh new tans, the weary looking businessmen with their briefcases. You could tell by the looks on everybody's faces that they were ready to get home.

When the plane was just about full, two men in their early thirties boarded together and sat down directly in front of me. As the plane started to taxi away from the terminal, I glanced up from the magazine I was thumbing through and noticed that the two guys sitting in front of me were kissing. Now, I don't mean they were giving each other pecks on the cheek; I mean they were kissing each other square on the mouth. And one of them was running his hand through the other one's hair. My first thought was, "I wish my cousin Doodle was here." You see, Doodle is a great people watcher himself, and I knew that there was no way he was going to believe this.

The hugging and kissing continued all the way through take-off. The captain finally turned off the no-smoking sign and I lit a cigarette. One of the lovers in front of me immediately stood up and said, "You're going to have to put that cigarette out."

"I beg your pardon?" I said.

"My friend Pinky finds it offensive," he snapped.

I said, "Let me see if I understand you. Is this the same friend Pinky that you've been hugging and kissing on the mouth?"

"Of course," he said.

"And he finds smoking offensive?" Before he could answer, I added, "Sir, my name is John Blanchard and I'm with the FAA, and it is my duty to inform you that there will be no more hugging and kissing on this airplane between you and your beloved Pinky."

"And why not, may I ask?" he said.

"Sir, in case you haven't noticed, you are in the no-kissing section, and need I remind you that according to the FAA code section IV, subsection D-4, unmarried passengers are not allowed to hug, kiss, pet or breathe heavy unless they are in the huggin', kissin', pettin', and heavy breathin' section of the aircraft? If you insist on continuing your vulgar display of public affection, I will, of course, have the captain slap you in irons and put you in the cargo hold of this airplane."

Pinky spoke for the first time, tugging at his friend's sleeve. "Oh, let him smoke, Hershel. Can't you see he's crazy?" Hershel quietly sat down.

I thought to myself, I'm glad my cousin Doodle isn't here. He never could keep a straight face.

The Best Years
Of Our Lives

The human mind is a little like an old-fashioned well pump: If you prime it just a little bit, the memories will soon start to flow.

One cold morning many years ago, my mother was trying to get me awake enough to go to school. I said, "But, do I have to go?"

She took a deep breath and said, "You don't know it now, but your school days will be the best days of your life."

I remember thinking, "Boy, is that a crock. I don't believe a word of it. That's just something they taught her to say to me in Mother School. How could these possibly be the best years of my life?"

The more I thought about this incident, and the wise, true words of my sainted mother, the more I thought about the wonderful days of my early school years.

The best thing about precious memories are that they do, indeed, linger.

I had been daydreaming only a few minutes when my entire grammar school career was as clear in my memory as today's breakfast. I remembered how proud I was of my new yellow raincoat with the hood. It looked just like the one policemen wore. I wondered if anyone would think that I was a policeman. Boy, I hope so. I remembered the rubbers my mother made me wear. They took hours to put on and take off, and besides, they made me look like a sissy. Why was it so important to keep your feet dry anyway? I had seen Gene Autry and Hopalong Cassidy walk in the water, and God knows, it didn't hurt them.

I remembered the new lunch boxes. My mother took me to Woolworth's to buy mine. She said I could have any kind I wanted (they all cost the same). My little mind was boggled. How could I ever decide? There was a Roy Rogers lunch box with a big picture on the side of Roy and Trigger, and sure enough, old Trigger was standing on his back legs. Did I want that one? How could I possibly pass up the one with Flash Gordon on it? The choice was impossible. There was the one with the Phantom and his pet wolf, Devil. Sitting next to it was Jungle Jim, Superman, and President Roosevelt. It took a while, but I finally chose the Lone Ranger and Tonto. I remember thinking as we walked out of Woolworth's, "The masked rider of the plains would sure be proud of me if he only knew that I chose his lunch box over all the rest."

That same night, my mother tried to buy me a Dick Tracy book satchel, but I explained to her that only sissies and girls carried book satchels. I was not a girl and God in Heaven knew I didn't want anybody to think I was a sissy.

The memories continued to roll. The new pencils, my very own crayons, a notebook. Keeping up with my own milk money. I smiled as I realized that I am no better at keeping up with money now than I was then. I remembered recess and all that went with it: swings, see-saws, tag, and "keep away."

I remembered the ultimate teacher's threat, "I will send you to the principal's office." It was common knowledge that the principal had a board with a nail in it, and if you were sent to the office he would spank you with it. And there was nothing your mother or anybody else could do about it. You knew that the principal was above the law and was allowed to abuse children at will.

I remembered the little girls in their new dresses (never jeans, never slacks, and never, never shorts). The dresses were freshly starched and always seemed to have bows in the back. I remembered the other little boys who, like me, wore corduroy pants that rubbed together and made a whistling sound when we walked. Whenever I wore corduroy, my granddaddy called me "Whistle Britches."

I remember the school safety patrol. We called them simply Patrol boy. It was a sad day in my young life when they allowed girls to be on the school safety patrol. I thought they were tampering with the natural order of things.

I remember the big silver radiators and standing beside them on rainy days, trying to dry off. I don't guess anything smells much worse than wet corduroy drying.

I remember the bully. He was always bigger than anybody else because he had failed at least one grade. I'll never forget the stories of the truant officer, and how if you "laid out" of school, he would come get you and send you off to reform school.

I remember the ultimate punishment, being kept after school. I remember the Christmas season at grammar school — the songs were learned, the Christmas tree, the Christmas pageant where the three wise men wore towels around their heads. What a special joy Christmas in grammar school was (damn you, Madeline Murray O'Hare).

I remember swapping valentines on February fourteenth. If we had been good, we always got heart-shaped cookies.

I remember our morning pledge to the flag followed by a Bible reading (Let's have two more "damn you's" for Madeline Murray O'Hare).

I remember candy pullings, paper sales, and the Red Cross drive. I remember saving stamps, war bonds, and air raid drills. I remember "Our Weekly Reader" and the joy and knowledge it brought to my life. I remember dusting erasers, asking to be "excused," tattletales, and taking names.

I remember the God awful lies we told when we didn't have our homework: My dog ate it; my little brother lost it; my mother died and I had to go to the funeral and didn't have time to do it. I remember learning to read about Alice and Jerry and their dog Spot. I remember a winter coat that my mother assured me I would grow into. I remember deficiency slips, tests, and report cards.

I remember the metal policeman in the middle of the street holding a sign that said "Slow School Zone." I remember the Tuesday morning chapel program. I remember being allowed to go to the library. I remember May Day; it was a great day at school till the Commies screwed it up. I remember the terror involved in going to the board when you knew you didn't know how to do the problem.

I remember the questions the teacher would ask: "Is that a yo-yo in your pocket?" "Would you like to let the whole class read that note?" "Did you bring enough gum for everyone?"

I remember the joy of learning, the laughter of the other kids, and the always warm days of my grammar school days.

The best years of my life? You betcha!

Wit & Wisdom From Ludlow

‘Never wrestle with a pig. It gets you all dirty and the pig likes it.’

*

‘My struggle to remain healthy is killing me.’

*

‘The trouble with being poor is that it takes up all your time.’

The Sandwich

I have always loved sandwiches. If my mother had not insisted otherwise, in all likelihood I would have grown up eating nothing but sandwiches and potato chips.

I have dedicated many years of my life in pursuit of the perfect sandwiches. I know what a sandwich is supposed to look like, feel like, smell like and, what's more important, taste like. If the federal government ever appoints a sandwich czar, I certainly will be a front-runner for the job.

The wonderful thing about a sandwich is that you can put almost anything you want to on one. I have eaten things on sandwiches that would cause a dietician to have a running fit. The only two things you must have for a good sandwich are fresh white bread and mayonnaise; if you don't care for them, then you have my deepest sympathy, for you are doomed to a lifetime of poor to average sandwich eating.

Once you have established in your mind that you start with white bread and mayonnaise, a whole new world opens to you. Your only choice from this point is to decide what other wonderful things you want. You can start with bananas and, if you like, add peanut butter. You might want to try just onion; it is a true delight. You may want to try my very favorite: thick sliced bacon, a slice of home-grown tomato, and some lettuce if you are on a health kick. Three meals a day, you cannot do better than a BLT.

If you have more rural leanings, you might want to go with a CLT. That's chittlin, lettuce and tomato. If that sounds bland, try chittlin, lettuce, onion and tomato. You call that a CLOT.

No matter what your taste calls for, you are never far from being full if you are a true sandwich eater. They will not only keep you from being hungry, they also will keep you from being lonely. How can we be lonely while eating? If you don't believe me, just ask any fat person.

When I finally am called home, I hope somebody will inscribe my tombstone as follows: "He crossed the river Jordan with a sandwich in each hand."

It Still Beats Me

I long ago decided that there are some things in life that I am not supposed to understand. I don't mean the big things, like how to make a trip to the moon or Algebra I. I mean simple, everyday things that I should be able to figure out but, for the life of me, can't. Let me give you a few examples:

Everytime we have a big election in this country, the newspapers are full of stories about the huge campaign debts of the losers. The next thing we hear is that somebody is giving a big fund-raising dinner for the fellow who went into debt while losing an election.

Now, that's a good and proper thing to do, and I have no problem whatsoever with it. My question is this: Why do we never hear about a benefit to pay off the winner's debts? It obviously costs as much, if not more, to win an election than it does to lose one. So how does the poor winner pay his debts? That could be a question we're better off not knowing the answer to.

I have never understood prom parties. Do you

remember how they were? You stood around and drank punch that you didn't like, trying to display manners that you didn't have. When you were ready to throw up from too much punch, you got to take a girl on a prom. That meant a walk around the block. Nothing happened, you just walked around the block. I went to many prom parties in my time, but I don't know why I kept going back, because your average prom party is about as much fun as unloading a dishwasher.

Why do airlines say they had a "near miss" when we all know what they actually had was a "near hit"?

Why do newspapers say that somebody in a wreck "barely escaped death"? They never say when someone is killed that they failed to escape death, or had a tie with death.

Why do Hershey's with almonds cost the same as Hershey bars with no almonds?

Why does the Professional Air Traffic Controller's Union use the word "Professional"? Are we to assume that somewhere in our great land there is a group of amateur air traffic controllers?

Why do traffic reporters refer to all streets other than expressways as surface streets? I thought, except for a few tunnels, all streets were on the surface.

Why do grocery stores put signs in their windows that say, "On sale, 'Homo Milk,' 79¢ a quart"?

Why does the highway department put up signs that say, "Bridge may ice in winter"? Seems to me that most folks know that dang near everything may ice in winter.

Why do radio stations say they are going to play ten "hits" in a row, and then come in after every record to assure you that you are hearing ten hits in a row? Then they give the station call letters, the time, the temperature and where your dial is set before they go back to the music.

Why do you need a license to fish, but you don't have to have one to drink whiskey?

Why do they call a glove compartment a glove compartment?

Why do gas stations lock their bathroom? What do they think you're going to steal?

Why do people at drive-in windows tell you to "Drive around please"? Do they think you're going to wait there for your food?

What is in McDonald's special sauce, and when are they going to McShut up about it?

Why do football coaches always refer to themselves as "we"? "We are expecting big things for our boys." "We try to develop men." "We enjoy coaching." Makes you wonder if they're pregnant, doesn't it?

Yes sir, there are a lot of things that I'm still trying to figure out.

The Truth About Apathy

My uncle, Seth Porch, was the happiest man I ever knew. I don't ever remember seeing him when he wasn't smiling. He was even tempered, loving, and managed to get through life by never sweating the small stuff.

In the middle 1930's, Uncle Seth was approached by some local men who wanted him to join the Ku Klux Klan. Seth said, "Why would I want to join the Klan? I'm already an Elk and a Mason, and that's about enough meetings for anyone to attend."

One of the men said, "But don't you want to keep the blacks from taking over?"

Seth laughed and said, "Takin' over? Most blacks I know are having about as hard a time as I am makin' ends meet. Besides, if I leave them alone, they're gonna leave me alone, and whatever they decide to do is none of my business."

When the war in Vietnam was in full swing, somebody asked Seth what he thought about our involvement. Seth scratched his head and said, "I don't know too much about it, but it seems like a right long way to go to mind somebody else's business."

The board of Deacons at Seth's church once called a special meeting to discuss the length of the new pastor's wife's skirts. She was not wearing mini skirts by any means, but some of the ladies of the congregation felt that decent women had to wear their skirts a certain length, and they agreed that the pastor's wife must set the "proper" example.

Seth let all the other deacons talk, and when it was his turn, he stood up and said, "The pastor is a good man; he works hard for dang little money. I figure the way his wife dresses is her business and not mine. Now, I suggest we adjourn, go home, watch Perry Mason and, from now on, try to mind our own business".

The dictionary defines apathy as (1) lack of emotion or feeling; (2) lack of interest in things generally found exciting, interesting or moving; indifference.

Uncle Seth defined it as minding your own business.

I'm with Uncle Seth.

Is That Ham
All Right?

Whenever there is any king of problem in America, a hue and cry goes up from those affected. They scream out as one, "Somebody ought to pass a law. The government should do something." Well, a while back, the government did do something. Let me tell you about it.

A few years ago, passenger train service was in trouble. The railroads were losing money hand over fist, so the government came up with Amtrak. Now the government was going to run our passenger trains.

Like most people, I don't get to ride trains as much as I once did. The pressures of my business cause me to fly almost everywhere I go. But I have very fond memories of train travel. I was, therefore, tickled nearly 'bout to death when a year ago, I had the opportunity to take a round-trip by train from Atlanta to New Orleans.

I had wonderful memories of the old Southern Cresent taking me to New Orleans and looked forward to doing it all again. We got on the train at 7:30 A.M. The first thing I noticed wrong was the conductor. The uniform was okay, but the hat was not right. It was just not a real, honest-to-God conductor's hat. It looked more like something a World War II pilot would wear.

The conductor also did not have gray hair. Thinking back to the good old days of train travel, I could not remember ever having seen a "real" conductor who did not have gray hair. How in the name of Casey Jones could you expect a conductor to conduct with that funny pilot's hat and no gray hair?

I was so enthusiastic about the trip, however, that I decided to overlook this government worker's impersonation of a real conductor.

Inside the train was mass confusion. The passengers did not know where to sit, and the government workers assigned to take care of that sort of thing were milling around as confused as everybody else. It took about forty-five minutes and, through some miracle that I can only attribute to Divine Intervention, we all found our assigned seats. My stomach told me that it was time for breakfast, so we made our way to the dining car.

The dining car was not the way I remembered, either. The tables and chairs were gone. The snow-white tablecloths were gone. The vase with the single, fresh flower was gone. And, Dear Lord, say it ain't so Johnny Cash, those wonderful dining car waiters with their crisp, clean, white jackets were gone.

The tables and chairs had been replaced with plastic modular booths that had obviously been purchased at a Burger Doodle going-out-of-business sale. They were uncomfortable, they were too small for any adult human, and they were ugly. No table cloth, no vase, and no flower.

The dining car was full for breakfast, and the government had managed to find two women, who had obviously been Nazi prison camp guards, and made them into what they hoped would pass as waitresses. They barely passed as earthlings. It seemed to take forever, but finally one of them came to our table and said in a flat, cold voice, "Are you people ready?"

I said, "Yes, do you serve grits?"

She said, "Did you see them on the menu?"

"We haven't seen a menu," I said.

She gestured toward a four-by-four card in a plastic holder sitting on the table. Then she snarled, "I'll be back when you've written down your order."

We checked the very limited menu and finally wrote down our order on the pads that the Nazi lady had provided. Our breakfast was served in square styrofoam plates. The coffee in styrofoam cups. The utensils were plastic. The juice came in a plastic cup with aluminum foil glued to the top. It was not the worst food I have ever seen, but I felt then, and feel now, that it would have caused a riot if it had been served to the inmates on Devil's Island.

The waitresses were scurrying up and down the aisles, and on one occasion, one of them bumped into my knee. She said in a loud voice,

"You're gonna have to keep your knee out of the aisle, fella!" I thought that must be the way they teach government workers to say, "Excuse me."

When breakfast was over, we made our way back to our seats. I read for a few minutes and then lay my head back on the seat and closed my eyes. The only sound that I was aware of was the clickedy-clack of the rails. It came to me suddenly that the only thing remaining of that wonderful old Southern Cresent was the clickedy-clack of the rails. As I sat there, my mind rushed back to the days before the government "saved" our rail travel.

I remembered another trip I had taken on the Southern Cresent. My bags were carried on board by a very friendly man wearing a red cap. He checked my ticket and took me to the right car. He told me what seat I was to sit in and, as I was getting on board, he said, "I hope you have a safe trip and I'll look forward to seeing you when you get back to Atlanta."

I passed the conductor and he smiled and said, "Good morning! Nice to have you with us."

We pulled out of the station right on time. Nobody announced that it was time for breakfast. You knew it because, by now, the aroma of biscuits, ham, and bacon was making its way throughout the length of the train. I was met at the door of the dining car by the dining car steward, a well groomed man in his middle to late thirties. Smiling, he said, "Two for breakfast, yes sir, right this way."

The dining car was furnished like a fine restaurant. Wooden tables with high-back chairs, and lots of room between tables so you never felt crowded. Our table was covered with a snow white table cloth. There were silver salt and pepper shakers, a vase with a single carnation, and silver knives, forks and spoons. There was a cup and saucer. Written on each in small, but proud red letters were the words, "Southern Railway."

Our waiter was at the table only seconds after we sat down. He was a tall, distinguished black man. He was carrying a silver coffee pot with a very ornate "S" on it. He was smiling as he poured our coffee. He handed us a two-page breakfast menu and said, "Mr. Porch (he had taken the time to know my name), I'll be right back to get your order and answer any questions you may have."

I had ham, eggs and, yes, praise be to Robert E. Lee, they brought me grits, and I didn't even have to ask. When I was about one-third through my breakfast, our waiter stopped by the table and said, "Mr. Porch, those eggs look a little too done."

I said, "No thanks, they're just fine."

"Are you sure?" he said. "I'll be glad to get you some more if they're not just the way you like 'em."

While he was there, he poured us some more steaming, hot coffee. When he brought us our check, he also brought us the Atlanta morning paper. He said, "Thought you might want to see what's going on in Atlanta while you're out of town."

In the middle of the afternoon, we went to the club car to have a drink. We sat down on a large, comfortable sofa, and within seconds a waiter was there to take our order. He repeated the same fine service we had enjoyed at breakfast.

When we got off the train that night in New Orleans, we felt that we had been traveling with friends. We were not tired, because the wonderful folks on the Southern Cresent had worked hard to see that our trip had been a fun, relaxed experience. They took pride in their jobs, they were good at what they did, and it was apparent that they enjoyed it.

The defenders of Amtrak say that if the government had not stepped in, there would be no more rail travel.

I take a different view. I think the Southern Cresent should have been treated like an old, dear friend, and allowed to die with her dignity intact, not taken over by a crowd of government workers who not only don't know how to run a railroad but have no desire to learn.

Rail travel did not die in America, it was murdered. And the thing that hurts most is that they used our tax dollars to pay for the killing.

A Precious Memory

My wonderful mother never quite understood what I do for a living. She knew that I was on the radio everyday, but as a lady who spent her life working in a shirt factory, I don't think she really thought that radio was a sho-nuff job.

My family is made up of the least show-biz oriented folks in the world. They have never been very impressed with the fact that, thanks to radio, I have become somewhat of a public figure. I don't want to leave the impression that my mother was not proud of me. I was an only child, and the love between us grew everytime the clock ticked. She would have been proud of me if I had been an unemployed wino. She just didn't understand what all the fuss about her "baby" was.

One time, I took her out to dinner. Some people recognized me and asked for an autograph. When they left the table, my mother said, "Who were those people?" I told her I didn't know who they were. In a surprised tone of voice, she said, "How could you not know them? They knew you."

The only show-biz personality my mother ever expressed any interest in was the wonderful pianist Carmen Cavalaro. She would tell you in a flash that no one on earth could play a piano like him. The only phonograph records she ever bought in her life were his. If she knew he was in a movie, you could bet that she was going to be there. When he was on "The Ed Sullivan Show," no one was allowed to talk until he had finished playing. My mother came very close to being a Carmen Cavalaro groupie.

When I heard that he was going to be playing at a local supper club, I called my mother and asked if she would like to go have dinner and hear him perform. She said it would be wonderful, and then she said, "Are you sure you can afford it? That's a pretty swanky place."

When I called for our reservation, the manager of the supper club said, "I listen to you everyday, and I will see that you have a good table."

When we arrived at the supper club, the head waiter sent for the manager, who came at once and welcomed us personally. He told my mother what a talented son she had and generally made a fuss over me. Not understanding what all the fuss was really about, my mother just smiled politely.

The manger said, "Mr. Porch, I have reserved three tables for you to choose from. One table is at ringside, another table is situated so you will have a better view of Mr. Cavalaro's hands as he

114

is playing, and one table offers your party more privacy." We chose the ringside table. Before the manager left us, he said, "Would you like to meet Mr. Cavalaro?"

I assumed he meant did we want to go back stage after the show, so I said, "That would be nice. My mother is a big fan."

In about five minutes, I looked up and standing at my table was the manager of the club and Carmen Cavalaro. I stood up and shook his hand, then I introduced him to my mother, who was absolutely speechless. He kissed my mother's hand and tears came up in her eyes as she said, "You're the best there ever was."

Later in the evening, while Mr. Cavalaro was playing, I noticed the tears rolling down my mother's cheeks. I said, "Are you O.K.?"

She kissed me on the cheek and said, "You have made me so happy, and so proud to be your mother."

Since I have been on radio, I have received much love and praise, a lot of awards that I didn't deserve, and generally have had a wonderful career. But nothing ever came close to that moment.

My mother and Mr. Cavalaro are both gone now, and someway, somehow, I hope they know that on that long ago night, they teamed up to give me a memory that I will always cherish.